LATHER YOUR WOUND IN SALT & LIME

A collection by Haley Vuleta

To Grandad & my past self, the

pillars of my life

Contents

"We all have an unsuspected reserve
of strength inside that emerges
when life puts us to the test."
-Isabel Allende

Fawn

WE THE RABBITS HAVE TEETH

Bronze, iridescent, the kind of pearls you swirl in the basin, a wispy brush sweeping along cheeks. There are flecks of powder scattering the countertop and smudged with liner, red stamps in a row and you're not sure which stick to choose for the day. What would go nicer on my lips, what could fit in my purse of the day, to be shared around as a baton, a trophy, a kiss of good luck. And you stagger out the door with a face fully carved, with lines like swords that sharpen, fending off the cat callers.

The wind latches onto the satin skirt that is wrinkling and billowing, fluttering a train behind and wrapping around your legs. *Jumping,* the tulips are humming, through the rigid fencing that files down the alley, into something more of harmony. You spy the man who waits idly at the traffic light, whose board has been battered and beaten, and he rides it through the street. Ignoring the lighted figurine as it flickers red, red, green, green. He glances around to see the spectators of his wicked demeanour; the tulips close their eyes.

Smiles turn the corner faster than you, they dabble down the cobblestones leading the final stretch. You pass the leaves that fester and crunch, abseiling from above, twinkling through the light, fraying at the edges. Should they catch ablaze, step aside.

There are textbooks peeking at you, their heads are perched on zips, in bags, in hands and they think for a while; how nice it is to have some air. Silver linings with fingerprints, hands that grab the rail and lurch it forwards and into and beyond. Students dancing the *cha cha cha,* as doors fling and exhale, ceasing the day and rippling down the quad.

Maui is lurching at the sun and it begs to the west, hurtling down the strip and reading; blue,

yellow, lavender, pink. And eventually it will go grey,
but you can't think of it yet with its candle-lit glow.
To be is to whoosh and away with it. And flashing
in the masonry striped tower is the clock that chimes
of fatigue. Assembling its jigsaw and hollering *au
revoir!* See you all next time, to win the game chased
as a rabbit in the race,

by the hounds with gritting teeth

that bite your nails to the quick and retreat.

MY JIGSAW RESIDENCE

Rhapsodic balconies and highly idealist waters are the sights I see from the steps.

A geometrical horizon of cubism,

        shapes all too unfamiliar and
    parallel between hills.

What a miracle that out of these

small

large

rigid

flat squares

unfold world after world after world.

A world that sings to you, tumbling down the hay-stricken grass, rejoicing to the daisies, the taste of springtime, the sound of syrup. Then the other, the one that exhilarates you, defies you, cheats you, the endless opportunities of quashing rebellion. How suave it is to live these worlds simultaneously, breathing recklessly into an ode, sprinkling my confetti, in hope that I too taste like clouds and the underside of a coin.

COMPLETELY FINE

November fell out of my diary like a pressed flower.

It slipped from the pages like a forgotten phone number riddled in a voicemail. It was during this time that I leapt through boulders childlike and uncanny, across the desert and buried deep into decorative passageways. Still, the most rooted moments were the journeys through my own multifaceted deliria, an interview of myself by myself and to myself.

I fell in love quite a bit, with quite a bit. That's if we're measuring in milestones and not in teaspoons. I stopped at the zebra crossings like it were second nature and held up my 'for sale' sign with pride and abundance, striking smiles as if it were desirable to others. Decades of disposing myself into the wretched bins of agony, I came from the ashes and tipped my tin hat to the bystanders.

Enacted in me a change of being and I came to one simple formula that is: *Lathering your wounds in salt and lime will not help. Not at all.*

So I've decided to break my own arm and let it heal with the lucrative touch of others, to mend my stitching with the overflowing amount of joy I witness on a school playground. People often fumble side by side and beg you to partake in their sonder activities, so perhaps instead of getting lost in the darkness, I will furnish a wealth of coloured joy.

AN ODE TO REBELLION

The tongues I tore from my ex's friends wriggle about indefinitely. They sing sweet-nothings and barricade my traumas like seashells, lining the shore and reclining. Like every romantic, I store one in my purse to revisit in a months' time, handing one to a lover as compensation, or forgiveness. The sea has a way of rising from the hollows, unhinging at the worst of times. Fixing on a flat white like some tiger in need of swagger, and other adjectives, the sand unapologetically becomes blind, crispy, and runs with the wind. I won't pretend to be a person anymore. Instead, I'll be a granule found in chia seeds, mulched in your puddings, a coordinated omen of destruction. Instead, I'll be an enjambement, a fall-off-the-edge kind of person. A wasp in pollination season, incubating my anger softly and in private, layering my resistance, my own weapon molecule by molecule. Instead, I'll be many things, anything but the person you want me to be. A person who bites, who abandons and stings without reason, because I know you would hate it.

FRIDGE MAGNET

How bittersweet it is to know him, between my legs and in my head.

How daring and wise it is to love him so thoughtlessly.

Love is terrifying.

HEARTBREAK HILL

Sometimes it is enough to close your eyes and taste the tears of disappointment.

All those nights with the car up the hill, sitting on the bonnet and looking out to the city sparklers.

All that liberation of talking and talking about journeys, humanitarians and things we wanted to do.

Lips that turned dark and eyes flickering through the headlights, kisses left on cheeks and hands that interlocked and caressed the space between us.

Nights are different, a reality that cannot be grasped because we spend so much of it inept.

A space where we craft our deepest thoughts and longings, wishful thinking that drops from the sky like confetti. Hoping that tomorrow we'll sit as changed beings.

We drove up the gravel as if it were the last time

closest to the clouds and moulding a frame of
where we both wanted to be.

But the sky festered into a sore, and we stayed to
see the warmth glowing up from the hills and
saying; *gidday, what are your plans for the day?*

And we realised we had none, so we exhausted
every store of conversation we had and tumbled
down to civilian life. Like we hadn't just spent an
entire night.

For there is nothing more vulnerable than someone
holding heartbreak in their hands,

a puppeteer twisting your ropes together and
leaving you there to hang.

2AM

The worst part was when I started loving you

I stopped liking you.

I was trapped in the reigns

that bound me into pain

I knew I couldn't leave

because it would ruin me. And I hated you for it.

SEASONAL

A poignant and uplifting autumn

striking

just the right balance of orange tone and feel.

A row of long sash windows

lime green tendrils of wisteria

dashing

along the wrought-iron gate

across a border in the distance.

To be awash in trivialities in a world so feathered,

I am amused.

NATURAL DISASTER

The weight of the world is competition

     under the burden of patience and inequality

     of failure and rejections.

The fight for survival is thin and melting like

icebergs sinking and quivering under pressure.

There's no attainable desire and we try to cultivate a

reality beyond reach.

     Blasphemy! We send our soldiers to the

moon whilst rejecting our own sphere

and we kill ourselves. We wait for the clock to tick

for our turn.

Rolling through new generations like an Oreo

packet, picking them apart and only eating the good

ones

the ones with the thick white icing.

There is havoc on the main road, smoke swarming
through cities like the plague

with masks like knives, standing guard and
rendering conflict.

Signs wavering through crowds with perpetrators
who are blind and ignorant

rendering conflict through standing guard.

Blasphemy! The maple syrup summer is
heating and gleaming in red, those who are lucky,
flee. It's a pity little miss cockatoo cannot escape to
sea.

Teenage Matrimony

POUND

What is it about the apparition of

a carefully crafted Mars bar,

that gives me intrusive thoughts.

ANGEL EYES

four

that's how old she was when they started her on
ritalin and trimipramine.

when she started punching holes through her
bedroom wall

jumping out the window

climbing on the house.

that's how old she was when they stripped her
naked and pried the childhood out of her.

ringlet curls and a pacifier were supposed to be
protectors, with a metaphysical caution tape
reading: *she is a baby*.

I suppose the next decade were the years of vicious
repetition,

of broken glass and bleeding legs, escapades from
the balcony and a warming to the DHB.

how pitiful that she spent years forging sanity out
of insane and begging for life to

just start over.

WASTE OF SPACE

He was wet socks and soggy cigarettes at the bottom of the glovebox, and hardly recognisable amongst other things. My pretty name came out of his mouth like a cotton ball, fluttering away, deuced in petroleum and set on fire.

THE RIGID TRUTH OF ADOLESCENE

We were never at peace. The voices inside our heads became our friends, after a long day at Blackbarn we'd trudge home to the screams beckoning us. We'd skip with hands in our hair, the golden orbs on our sunglasses gleaming into the light. It wasn't enough to sit quiet like an abscess, festering and crusting, waiting to heal. Volume is all we had, the kind that is transfixed and commentating on running races, the kind that steadies the fist in your hand, the kind that leaves the hummingbird to quiver. I spent my teens hacking at gilitines that looked like razors, pushing my body through depths of water until I lost control and floated back up. I ripped paper like it were old news and Hitler propaganda, glass slicing through inches of thigh, hyperventilating in my bedroom and sharing the space with demons. I counted carpet fibres like it were competition, tweaking and jittering, pressing my body against the locked door and screeching until my vocal cords tore. I spent a lot of time not knowing how to breathe, confined in small words and the writing I had in my notebook. I started drinking black coffee, it gave me hope, it saved me, it saved all of us.

FRIENDSHIP SYRUP

A wine bottle has a lot to teach us.

It ripens with age well beyond its years, bottled wisdom.

Opening the bottle is a choice in solitude or with company,

a drink to be shared, celebrated, sung to, cried in.

It is there for all your triumphs and falls.

It will make you

fall in love,

fall sleepy,

fall impaired.

It is yours to ponder over, a listener to your long day.

Don't be fooled by its magnitude strength; it is fragile and will break easily.

So, tread carefully, hold tightly and seek refuge if need be.

WHO MIGHT BE

I am Dylan Thomas in America. A drunken poet enriched in the stale bars, the crooked sidewalks and bouncing between readings. Teeth like mothwings, fingers frail and cracked from cigarettes lodged in between. Witty yet earnest, commanding intimate attention yet wanting none of it. Living life in solitude alongside pints of stout. New York's correspondence, a silhouette in the city lights, a nobody but everybody all at once. Shoes with laces dragging behind, cuffed leather, the kind that is sanded by the winds of change and walking uneasy paths. A belligerent conversationalist, words that are parachuted to become part of history. A troubled soul, in conflict with himself and others, a catalyst for his craft. Slowly the city puts his soul to sleep and I am at peace with the prospects of my derailing psyche.

For Jane Austen

BYGONES

To be completely devoid of sentiment is like
mottled ice and pebbles.

Entering in a new world, pink-flowering thorns and
heavy scented lilacs.

The door widening by the proletariat, grasshoppers
chorusing up the wall.

I suppose in our madness we have separated the
two, invented a realism so vulgar,

an ideal void.

Sitting in the tussocks and plainland, the wonder I
had always looked for

was suddenly become by a lifeless appearance,

fearless

unacquainted

nothingness.

I will not bare my soul to their shallow prying eyes.

My heart shall never be put under that microscope
– again!

I suppose they know how useful passion is for
publication and how many editions I will exhale
within my lifetime.

Many delinquent dandelions will be trod and
mulched to brick,

an ornament for summer.

So, I let the ambiguous encircle me, honey-
coloured chrysanthemums that somehow seem still
and non-confronting.

GARDEN THINKING

The leaves conjure into the vines and spiral into a woven city.

I watch the branches circle into a road and lead each other in the same direction.

The light twinkles from up above, catching the crisp of the leaves and wavering off the edges. If you sit under the canopy, you will only see the tree trunk, a slab of bark standing upright.

The tree is towering, and you can't see the foliage or the leaves. The leaves are the best part, but you must stand up and walk away to see its full potential. It's the same with people, up close you only see the mediocre version of others, you paint a picture of a person by what they tell you. Yet there's so much more potential if you could only walk away, stand from a distance, and admire the beauty of a once simpler thing.

If you glance sideways,

you'll catch a glimpse of the geraniums; the peach
ice roses; the ones that stand in solitude blossoming
and flirting at the bumblebees.

But none of them are alone,

each organism is protected by something else; a flax
leave spread eagle, ivy curling down the fence,
hedges that border the grass and link with the
lavender, the daisies, the kauri tree. To the
untrained eye they all seem cluttered and bush-like,
an endless weed that wraps around the house
shielding from the predators.

But individually,

they have a purpose, to flourish, to feed from each
other, to be swarmed in a textured philanthropy.

OKAY (IN MEMORY OF MATT)

I saw the best minds of my generation looking out to the sky,

it was tinged with sadness and melancholy.

I watched the spirals fade from fluorescent red and melt into the black nothingness. Fireworks crackling to the sounds of rejoice and the new year anthem. It was enough to make my heart explode. In fact, it did at that very moment. I stood there on the hill watching the smoke sway over the sea, people huddled and jumping together. Fast forward a few days and I'm sitting on the church cues, scanning the crowd, crying. The same sadness echoing out to the black nothingness. He lay there confined in mahogany panels, timber lines running down the edge of the coffin and reaching the silver clips. So close to someone yet so far from it. Tears of loss and sadness became selfish, they wanted to see him again and be with him. I was more saddened by where he was and if he was okay. I wondered if he knew he was dead or if he fell into a void without conscience. I hoped he was put to rest with calm and ease. That's the thing about dying, we're obnoxious to think there is life after death, we want to believe that our small lives will never end. But they do. And we will never matter again and never get to walk another day, a day that we took for granted. A day where we complained about life and its terribleness, how awful it is, how draining it can be. But we wake up, we didn't ask to wake up. We don't know why we wake up, but we trot along going about our simple lives to enliven our minds and make ourselves feel somewhat enjoyable. We wait and pass each sunset, a day closer to our own death. The inevitable gap awaits us, and we are clueless about where we go. So, I say this to you Matt; I hope wherever you are, you are okay. You are calm and you find homage in the fact that you lived and ended this life as it were meant

to be, perhaps a little too early.

WHEN I FOUND ME

Bees are passengers in the wind, perfect petal
landings with cultivated pollen treasure.
Strawberries are strung from the fields and awaiting
pick, flaunting lavishly at passers.

These are the things which I have acquired;

my voice is lower,

my hair is lighter,

my posture is straighter, and my mind is so
exquisite I get lost in it often.

The trees are softer, they whisper to me now that
you are gone.

Because I captured my essence in a sailboat and
hitched a ride to Sicily,

the surge gravitated to a place of wonder,
navigating through turmoil and I knew the window
at dusk would light a path homeward bound.

Now everything I have is complete,

there is everything else and not much.

Just dandelions prancing in the grass, bent
backwards, embroidered in the stitching of the
ground.

BEPUZZLING

A fluffy bee scrambling an oval sphere

watching with the strange interest in trivial things

one might develop when afraid or bepuzzled.

Some new emotion we cannot find expression for.

In a white-walled prison one must reminiscence

and hold fast to those memories

roaming free in the mind that is both built and

cursed.

Stuck in a world of hellos and goodbyes, there is

love.

There has to *be*.

A DISREGARD

I hate happy people; I think they're silly and fucked. I don't hate the people that get excited or overjoyed or drunk. I hate the people that are happy all the time, for no apparent reason, smiling constantly like sunshine pours out from underneath the crevices of their ass cheeks. The happiness I cannot comprehend because I have no idea where it comes from, or how it goes away. But it does. That loud and cheerful grin and the do-good attitude fades, I suppose I know this to be true. These happy people are naïve and oblivious, wasting their energy on nobody's when they could be savouring it for the somebody's. I think energy is a wonderful thing to protect, however you don't realise it before it is taken away. The light washes from your face until it is grey and gaunt, slicing away from the inside out until your eyes begin to sag and it takes an army to affirm a simple, smile. It's like one day a switch flips, the humanity switch that cripples the fear and embarrassment inside of you, it cascades down your back like an oversized school bag and you lug it around. I don't know for how long. There is no eloquent resolution or frivolous rhyme for this poem for it has no ending. For I hate happy people, so perhaps I hate my past self, my past happiness, my past life.

CITY LUST

There are moments in the city where I feel more
like spun sugar than time.

A summer evening on a stretch of sand,

the first lick of an ice block,

watching a star shoot above the balcony,

a paranoid visionary in awe of his surroundings;
eating a bagel and contemplating his next creative
endeavour.

Or a hindered heartbeat

as the hummingbird touches the ground nearest to
you.

It's in the city that I find myself stopping at a body
of water;

one is somehow suspended and halted for a
moment,

a neutral being controlled in its own construct.

Through fascination comes an aspect of reflection,

through presiding in the existence of another –

come to think of it – we seek to know ourselves.

Something about looking out to the mass of blue,

unforsaken to the human eye and it stretches

beyond what we can comprehend.

A leap of faith can uncover what exactly is beneath

it,

a life-affirming domain that wisecracks its way

from dark to light and somewhere in between.

It's in the city I find I am not myself; I am all the

books I have read, all the men I have loved, and

every ounce of nature I have picked and marvelled

at.

So maybe it isn't about who we are and what we

see, but rather how we get there by the seemingly

miraculous entourage.

TEXTING WARS

It's a strange end to a never-ending war of words

I do love you and you didn't particularly fail

You set me back shunted out the door

You set me back to square one.

Grow up

attacking me for my deepest darkest secret

I'd rather one of us ended it before shit hit the fan.

I miss you sleeping on my chest

You made me cry you deserve so much better than
me

Fuck you.

THE IMPORTANCE OF BEING ERNEST

Poets – will love you like they fail to love themselves

tread carefully or they'll write about you.

We are inherently sad and earnest.

BRIDGETON EXPOSÉ

Razor blade wrists a swoon to the heir,

a puddle of lustre collects at thy feet.

A taut face has much to teach us bruised with
exhaustion,

gold coins eyes

one charitable mouth closing.

ONE LAST REPLY

Grief is forever wishing on an unspoken sentence,

picking up the phone

one last reply.

It is holding onto the 'I should've' with guilt and

shame.

It is spinning the wheel of time as the pain slowly

becomes distant

mending the stitching with a façade and hoping the

pretend will only

be a while.

It is counting to ten and drawing the clouds

looking up at the sky

as he looks down at me.

VALENTINE'S DAY

I am here staring at the red battery on my phone

awaiting that connecting abys

calling to do things unspeakable to me.

You monopolise my time.

ATONED

To whom do I owe the pleasure?

Mr Darcy, I am the string to your quartet in which

you pluck and pull at your disposal.

Oh how I adore you, Mr Darcy.

Wings aflutter grass is long hands are held.

So this is love…

two imperfect people always giving in to each

other.

Dirty Martinis

YOU, MY MAP

There are twelve worlds in your eyes, and I access them all at once. One I draw my muse from, others my passion and perseverance, one I use to harness my late-night endeavours; ponderings that continue until mid-morning. Then there's the last in which I live; the geographical counterpart where I reside and spend my time.

You are just two chocolate eyes away from melting me to tar

engraving me in concrete with a paw.

MANNERS

It's a polite dysphemism to say *go fuck yourself*. I quite like it; the raw sex appeal of the slogan is erratic and deferring. It could mean a multitude of different things.

I use it frequently.

BORROWED JUMPER

Russet clad and hugging

fitting the inches between you and I,

fending off your comments and

baring my scarlet letter.

26°49 (WHERE MAGNET ST IS)

By nine in the morning on a sultry summer day,

I no longer was mad that you didn't want me.

I was mad that you acted like you did

you had me wondering what it would be like,

to be burned alive along all my nerves and cease to

exist.

I thought it must be the worst thing in the world.

But perhaps as I sit at the marina surrounded by

macadams, I laugh in the place I once cried,

knowing you do not love me,

but I still hold all *my* love inside me.

COMING HOME

You as an empath, you know *you* are intuitive

those things are great

but how much of those things came out of trauma?

How much were programmed to abandon yourself

and be hyper aware of

every

single

subtle

signal

from everybody else?

Turn your empathy inward

It's time to come home.

OVERACHIEVING

The heist for success is exhilarating

like many that have come before

 the power of a talk show host, debilitating.

Yet they return back to their apartment on the

coast

fucking for hours like they both want to have a

heart attack,

and die together

that death-do-us-part type of shit.

It's the achievement of two people giving in,

establishing some form of equity like a miracle.

The heist to gain something is immeasurably

unattainable

isn't it enough to sit in solstice and want absolutely nothing?

Just the heart to tick

the brain to wire

the pencil to keep on sharpening.

TOXIC DESSERT

When Rihanna said she loves the way you lie, I felt that.

My cortisol hormone raging for the repeating cycle

what will it be today, validation or infuriation?

Serve me up a platter

thank you.

JUNE 3ᴿᴰ

The first frost of many,

the benches fickle frozen and laced,

skeletal leaves breaking on entry.

Turnips in the yard have not survived and I wonder

how I have.

My leaves are soon to shed.

26°49 (WHERE MAGNET ST IS) AGAIN

I want to press these nights between the pages of a
book and keep them forever.

This finite love and tardy lust

the backseat of my car

abrasive yet tender.

These kisses perorating me

keys locked within again

I feel somewhat at ease.

WRONG ONE

Spring-lit cheeks, silver swooning lashes and
sovereign smiles

often leave one so unromantic.

I picture it the same as my loved one buried

in cool geraniums,

feverishly drinking its perfume

like it were mine.

It's a shame she was bare headed with rebellious
curls, a communion tangled in gilded leaves. To
walk into a beautiful thing and be able to walk away
is something I wonder about the most.

Old-Fashioned

THE FIRST APPRASIAL OF MANY

My father looked upon me with such curiosity as with pride.

The swimmer manqué had brought forth the likened arms of Danyon Loader,

with powered legs that swelled and kicked through water,

beating all the boys.

Funny that, I'm always beating the boys.

EMBASSY

We called it the mansion, more so a shack but we'll excuse the latter.

Painted rust and grey,

perched above the house and a few yards from it; renaissance stone-walls and cobbles.

A balcony looked above bringing in sunlight and sea light,

shallows between long sloping hills – terminating to the harbour.

The interior; once cream, now grimy and ridden with mould,

weathered and speckled with who-knows-what.

Cans were tossed underneath rugs and couches, a keepsake for the next tenants-

it's how we liked it.

So long as we were together, nothing else seemed
to matter.

So long as we were drunk, no one else seemed to
exist.

HOME AWAY FROM HOME

If you asked me what life on mars looks like,

I'd tell you to sit on your window ledge

a cigarette in hand

looking up at the orange aperol sky. Squint like

you're just seeing it for the first time.

PRETTY LITTLE H-

Think it's time to spit the soap out of my mouth, to

do rather than die.

I think it's time to stop flirting with the window

ledge and close the shutters -

but oh it's so pretty down there.

The pavement needs decorating,

something new and something borrowed.

I think all these bombs inside of me will bleed out

down there.

 Pity no one sees my Armageddon, I'm smarter

now, older,

now this isn't copacetic. How collateral is that

shelf? I'm asking for a friend.

Just a pretty little thing who can't handle her drink,

who runs in front of cars in hope that they

blink.

FORGET ME NOT

An oblique relationship with reality

orbiting around in conversation,

entering each day an unfamiliar face.

The painting was once here, you know the one,

with the girl flying the kite?

Dreamy expressions harrowing, capturing

something elliptical.

Intimacy intruding night-goggles, tossing in the

sheets and waking every hour.

Something like being abrasive and unrestrained,

you make people uncomfortable

you know that right?

The fork you keep under the bathtub, the watch

walking in amusement of

time

wasting

slowly.

Drawing lines in the foreheads of strangers that
waltz in and out of this room.

The leaves are turning over but who's house is this?
It must be *mine* because I lived here once.

CONVERSING AT DUSK

The sky was cloth and birds ran over it in threads.

The grass was warm, with a smell all too allergenic
and familiar.

His hands were large and full of practicality, fitting
into mine like they needed fixing.

Those nights with the quiet complaint of the
headboard,

doors clicking shut,

the hum of two voices.

How fearlessly elicit the sugar plum nights were,

with an unmitigated awe drifting from his eyes
down to my hips,

fluid to my membrane, hopscotch on my heart.

MUM

The wetness of her face answered my question.

She talked then about riding a bicycle downhill,

getting to that exhilarating point where you don't
know whether the feet are pushing the pedals, or
the pedals are pushing your feet.

*I wanted my feet to be pushed into places they wouldn't
normally have been.*

Like making shapes out of glass,

she spoke with clarity that sounded like
disappointment.

Retreating from the gravel in agony,

a hip that needed replacing, feet to the medal and
tender cartilage.

GIRLS ARE OVERRATED

I suppose it's not what you can do for misogyny but what misogyny can do for you.

 In a world that begs for the French tip manicure and bombshell curls, one must wear the pants and be careful not to spill coffee onto them. Be bold they tell you, but not so bold to attract the wrong publicity, be a lady of effortless physique and smart enough to make money for yourself. But oh, don't overwork. Those bags under your eyes will be weighted with righteousness and narcissism.

I choose to rebel quietly, certainly I choose myself.

Over this.

For the rest of my life.

AFGHAN BISCUITS

The catastrophe —

locked out of house and home.

The rain goes down smooth and terribly, the feeling of someone leaving, the tap running sounds like gunshots.

The madness is deafening, the solstice that surrounds me broken by cries across the equator. Sometimes it's easier to pretend, but for whom?

My occipital fills with thunder and fog, thrashing conflict and screwed up fists.

Tyre marks in the gravel remind me of worse.

Far in the distance someone is eating copper and I can taste it in my mouth.

Transposing to the Aquarian age, I have Gaia to thank for these thoughts, intrusive and uninviting they are.

So instead, I'll sit engulfed in paper and books and marking and desks and tell the children not to go to the lake. I'll tell them to lock their doors and pray before bed and be good to their parents and walk in the thick shame of our world because nobody can go near the lake anymore. The lake that surrounds our entirety, that upheavals bodies from water, that strips our deeds and philanthropy away. So, we bite down on spoilt milk and curdle to the sound – the one that chimes at midnight and screams; *more lives are lost.*

SHOWER

Cross legged in the shower

eating droplets like it were cereal

wondering how did the tiles get

so cold.

BOOKSTORE LOVE

I think you knew she was different

when she looked at books with the same awe

capable of comfort

in ways you never saw.

BLANCHE

A grave start to an otherwise graceful morning.

Sealed in grey

with droplets hanging from winter trees.

Imposed before an expansive amount of space

a backdrop of bush and foliage

networked and

impressive.

PLEASE DO NOT HINDER MY MUSE

I keep books under my bed,

so I don't fall

off the deep end.

Laying adjacent and absorbing worlds of

romance and art

categories of my night-time land.

Pragmatism

CLOUDLESS TERRAIN

The morning seeps above the flat line,

littering only laughter and smiles.

Collecting memories, touching hands, sharing

boulders of my complacent heart.

Scouring for one more time, wilco, I'm saying yes.

I can feel it drill into my membrane and pour out

my ears, confronting every no, and irradicating.

I can hear my own name turning from grey to vivid

yellow.

Reaching out to touch me is sunshine and fleeting

eyes.

Hearing whispers in the birds, the ocean kissing my

ankles,

I'm invited in, and I intend to stay.

Many moons in the daytime roll over,

glistening porcelain teeth, lips supple under pressure.

My mind runs around the decade, searching for old heirlooms passed down by the hereditary brain wranglers.

Absent and peaceful thoughts, no one outside begging to be let in and destroy.

How blissfully peculiar that I have found wonder in a world so tethered.

PEAKY BLINDER

Iridescent sunrise turned violet

or to violence. One cannot distinguish which.

For they both have the same hue, both were once a

lilac shape and were licked to an outward

vengeance.

THE UNCONTROLLABLE

The vastness of the ocean has a way of making things and people seem insignificant.

A new perspective to see problems with, such freedom and autonomy the natural world holds.

Like a cloud hovering above water, dimming everything below it,

teasing a small space between sky and sea yet no one batters an eyelid.

It's hardly a quandary, becoming azure and finite.

IMMINENT

Flying over the cuckoo's nest

I nestle into the pragmatic, observant and sublime.

Stifled air complies most of 2021 except now.

I feel a wound of adoration bleed out

a way for the world to function.

Something about fleeting youth and

green tendrils of wisteria.

DEAR MY OLDEST AND LEAST FAVOURITE FRIEND

Thanks for playing this round of *Carpe Diem*.

I suppose I should thank you for repelling the academics and publishing the obscene odes on my windowsill.

Better which, for leaving your empty beer bottles on my rabbit cage.

A maddening hunger has much to teach us;

ivy clinging to branch, wrapping around, suffocating its entirety.

Reaching into the abysmal nothing, I know leaves do not have nervous breakdowns.

I believe in ordinary; I also believe in bravery, and one must succumb to the pressure of others in due force.

In the voice of rain banging on my roof, the howl of birds fleeting away from home, the whisper of grass torn from soil.

Do I dare strike out to find new grounds or stay buried as a hatchet awaiting the next clue?

GOLD CROWNED TEETH

We let honey drip from our tongues and spell out words of *amnesty* and *belligerence*. We stand on desks to gain new perspectives, towering over those inept to the jukebox.

Craving otherness; a dark rot that seems to stick with everything.

Something about doing things with people you're not supposed to. And as progressive as we are, last night's eyelashes are embedded in the pillow, crumbled black tar – the kind buried in lungs. Stuck in a world of optimists and pessimists, we grip each other's wrists like corsets, threading veins and threatening to make webs. It's like every time the world breathes, we breathe out all the oxygen we have – until there is none.

ROARING GALORE

Long, louche gourmandizing nights of bodies,

dancing in a rouge of 20s and 30s.

Together in lust and violence

at the end – drama in its stagnant and coldest form.

It seems to cast it's glance across the night, a flicker

of sentiment posed downward. Distasteful facts laid

out and through the looking glass we see that the

future of wild partying has been passed down by

the likes of *Bugsy Malone*.

In a world so fraught by constant threat and

frequent annihilation the *'eat, drink, and be merry*

because tomorrow may never come' is the only anthem.

Bottom-less cocktails, baritones, sequins, stained

lips, unending jazz, kissing crazes and -

an existential bag to pack.

Forgetting one's troubles is never out of style. It's
as if they know we don't pay attention to the
heedless scolding, and departing tabloids.

It's good isn't it,

grand isn't it,

swell isn't it

hell, I'd even say divine.

Nowadays you can live the life you want, without
wanting the life you live.

MOVING IS HARD

There are moments when the question of ends,
middles and beginnings

is literally life or death.

It feels more contemporary than ever.

Modern-day uncertainty, feeding on demise

like surf that retreats time after time

      perhaps never knowing real change.

Like cliffs that are trodden eroding heedlessly.

Recounted routes and horizons that seem to differ
in size

how do you say goodbye to a place of such certainty;

familiar hands

smiles

gestures revising new ones in the same didactic

manner

is tiring.

Leaving is non-linear it retreats, washes away,

repeats.

Maybe this time it'll be different. Maybe.

WELL MANNERED EXPOSÈ

To be the most extempore talker,

no doubt he was stimulated by his own demeanor

and wit.

The construction of his gesture is unlikeable.

Everybody else is solemn correct polite.

Smoking and cross legged, conducting himself

with irreproachable exactitude

hitching trousers before sitting down

moving hair and adjusting glasses.

Alas, everybody acts in a collective manner.

It is important to be well-mannered, in the same didactic manner we have copied from our elders, everything is passed down.

Everything depends on no one losing their temper or poise,

we must be smooth and stylish but not balletic.

Through delicate cadence, the intrinsic quality of

wit is revealed-

a niche for sophistication.

Nowadays you can't go anywhere without meeting

clever people.

The thing has become a public nuisance,

we have few fools left

to satisfy our goodness.

SMAILLS BEACH

What world does a dog know?

eager and boisterous shaking hands with a seal.

LIVED, LAUGHED, LOVE

A child lulled, resting in a wheat field

in love with all things made up, it's hard to imagine

the life you see for yourself.

Strolling in Brooklyn, folding over a napkin

encased with a kiss.

Romanticising the small things is crucial

without it we die trying.

Otēpoti

MIDDLETON ROAD

Essential places like my patio force me into balance

expressing terrain within cultural and sub-cultural surroundings,

the ivy the flax bush the tui.

Abnormality becomes my own multifaceted identity. The road climbing adjacent to papātaunuku meeting somewhere in-between ranginui

and the power pole.

In a constant state of transition, the world peels away from the marketplace and

into solstice.

PAINTING DAYS

canvas Sundays are pleasant.

delicately short

harmoniously timed.

colour boards seem to reminisce the week and roll
over -

painting bodies a luminescent frame tainted
nailbeds.

a brutally soft kind of day,

tucked beneath your shirt,

drawing clouds into your chest.

AGING

By the time I had been alive for 21 circumnavigations of the sun, I started dreaming of a world. Lazy disturbances in the night were suddenly – untethering. Taunted by the nightlight and creaks of the floor, I settled into myself as home.

Estranged from my final form, I never stop exploring

defining

becoming

changing.

I am alive and wheeling the motions of my own body, whistling through the leaves and the fingers cracked on the pavement, stretching far and long away in the distance.

WARPED BETWEEN PLACES

What do I owe this displacement? Somehow

feeling like a letter, stuffed,

ridiculed, thrown in the trash like a debt recaller.

Isn't it what we all venge for -

a place to sit at a table, among our loves and inept

from sorrow.

To have my heart divided is neither crushing nor

pragmatic.

One foot in, one foot out stretched and grown

wide.

DISPLACEMENT

I measure pieces of happiness

with analytic eyes;

I wonder if it looks like mine

weighs like mine

feels like mine.

I wonder –

did it arrive at the same time? Have they always had it, perhaps it's a recent thing?

A sense of place is important, to be divided and misplaced is most *unbecoming*.

COPS AND ROBBERS

And yet I gripped his slim

importuning hand

wondering how I became the villain.

FLYING FOX

a ruthless game on bare bark

flying through rope

with dangerous leg stranglers,

gripping and yanking

screaming for defeat.

the floor is lava

but don't tell anyone.

LAY ME HERE FOREVER

Love is lying in a dandelion field,

a warm bench to lean on

a light chest breathing feathers.

Every decision made with such finality and conviction

there are no what ifs.

My meta-being caressed and shown the way

its nearly impossible to doubt how capable I am for you tell me every day.

Love is lupins and lavenders spotting the road and leading to

a wide mountain range,

casted by sun and the promise of eternal light.

Beneath a veneer of old-fashioned love you are my comfort.

Exquisite and refreshing

nakedly looming and

staying here for good.

I AM HAPPY, I PROMISE

I suppose it is hard to capture the essence of

happiness,

in words it seems impossible.

Yet sadness has its own dictionary

it seems to last longer

penetrating deep

into saturated wounds.

Maybe happiness is more about enjoyment than

noticing.

To be felt rather than observed.

SUN KILLER

Impartial to the summer sun,

painkillers surround the loneliness.

Skyward herons seething,

All my soul is baring out in the noonday sun,

coconut oil igniting my sternum with pressing rays.

See, permafrost entombs most of me,

few can enthral me.

Pointing lights drool over my suburb, one day
they'll catch me.

For now I'll just sit inside, emancipated by the day's
feverish den.

HARSH BEGINNINGS

Your new year's resolution is sobering and
untamed.

How much sugar will infiltrate into your wound,

before you realise it is

salt.

SUMMER DIARIES

A flight of grey stone steps, leading somewhere and then nowhere.

In December, tables are covered in cloth beneath the canopy

wisteria lingering and keen to escape their post.

In January, children are skipping and holding fast to lavender memories.

This poem that I recall in summer, with twinkling teeth and extended hands

cannot be erased.

RAZOR SHARP CANALS

Insular somnolence, there is always war. Without it, we succumb to proxy.

A sturdy means of promise

adjacent to a war of ideologies principles negligence.

A war between two ways of understanding -

freedom alignment fidelity.

EPILOGUE

sometimes I miss my old self who I thought I was

miserable without her so maybe I am

still here.

Eggs & Soldiers

MY HERO

It's until I swallow death, in the window of my

recalcitrant town

that I realise - it's you who raised me.

It seemed like for once in this brutal life, I had

someone looking over me. More than a distant

relative – a dad.

Three and sun basking in Bondi, the child left on

your doorstep

became daughter, friend, someone to confide it.

Something we both had. You were hot sand and a

golden necklace; the one designed for your first-

born son. I always came first.

Your words unwrapped cloaks of opportunity, of

doing my best, staying off the drink, biggles.

I could always count on you.

Time expressed the space between us

and I had history to thank for your strings of wisdom.

You'll have to count on me now – agile, ambitious, draping the cloak of opportunity.

This one is for you Grandad.

2022

I can taste gunshot wounds and fear curdling
screams.

The erosion of memory

manipulated

by an atrophy of information.

Minds, bodies, and souls are decaying.

Why would I ever want to bring a child into this world?

Nowadays, unhappiness and isolation is the purest
form

of self-indulgence.

COMRADES & COMMODITIES

Each one moved along, intoxicated by solitude, by green and blue silence. The dazzling and secretive work of nature – a growing threat to encapsulation. Soldiers spared their livelihoods, whilst poets remained at home –

captured by their ambition their humanity their hurt.

It's not enough to stay buried as a hatchet.

Books are published at the same price of ice-cream and militias spend their entirety.

I picture these books – sun-drenched and parched, left outside barricaded abandoned burnt.

I suppose no one reads hardbacks anymore.

NO WAY OUT

Someone told gravity that we're all suspended

he laughed

tossing us deep underground.

Instead, we forgot what we were told

holding placards to the sky – perhaps as protest but

also in thanks.

For puppeteering us for a small while, long enough

to make friends withstand love, walk a mile.

We leave behind everyone who ever knew us, me.

Yet here I am, not much but still some

a rugged escape artist.

CHILDHOOD DREAMS

we ate sand and sung sweet lullabies.

we dressed our barbies into plastic and joked about
the future

what could we look like one day?

we rode our bikes into the gravel with stones
pressed into our knees

laughter dotted the streetlights and we had
company to thank for our adventures.

now

I sit in solitude listening to ice and wine mettle
together

seething and hissing

reminding me that life wasn't always this way.

CAFÉ STORIES

Tiny slivers of humanity rebrand themselves in gossip.

Whispers and consonants, a burst of voices and a snickering ear.

Each pair derived from a distant unknown life. Many lives are lived in this place.

We're connected in peculiar ways -

in

COFFEE. GOSSIP. LAUGTHER.

Rejoicing and sulking, looking down at coconut lattes and sipping away the times.

Whiskered grey and falling on all fours, this emotional energy is spent.

Our deeply rooted fears quarrels philanthropies are laid to rest and tucked in.

M'LADY

Fashion and adornment came about with just the right poise.

My ancestor stood defiant in a raging ribbon corset, hoisted by the renaissance. I imagine her scaling marble tiles and fleeting masquerades, loitering her thoughts into thin air.

She would flicker down the domain singing,

playing along with your riddles and wake before her counterpart,

with enough time to study his sleeping corpse and

write her own obituary.

My ancestor was equal parts clinquant and a sound raconteur.

She ought to be feared, and when she wasn't – she pierced her genes with that same anger and ambition.

So now you know,

centuries of analytic eyes and razor blades

exist in me.

THE SWEETNESS OF DOING NOTHING

Dolce far niente

peppered pillows and outside rain

the joy of living in fairy down.

SYBIL IN KHANDALLAH

At least with children, she felt brand new. An
abundance of new life as hers was ending. Through
the innocence, her face licked with age

accommodating the earth and modern battlefields.

She quickened the young with classic posture,
silver wear and chandelier jewels.

This is a cry of sorts.

A pine forest has been pat down, fastened and laid
to rest.

The wind now tastes of saw dust and syrup, a
divine entity of history and new beginnings.

In childhood, the church cue is rigid, hard stead a
lurking reminder to be upright and present.

In adulthood, it cushions the blow of the outside
world, cloud-like, candy floss, love and forgiveness.
It feels like fuchsia and smells of stain, a glorious

reminder that things are not meant to stay. She was
so far-fetched people travelled days to reach her,
perhaps it was her stamina, delusion, or rest-
assured peace. Carelessness of anything that did
not directly impact her. I suppose that kept her
alive for ninety-eight years.

Inept to anything apart from keep. yourself. alive.

An admirable copy of *mona lisa*, her frown lines
limited and conceited. She meant a lot to others,
naturally. So instead I should rephrase this
disposition - she was calcified hearts

and a road well-travelled.

She seemingly formed a cul-de-sac,

a turnaround

full circle

moment of greatness.

A homage for her grandchildren a configured
finger directed outward.

THROUGH THE PORTAL

Tight hugs and whimpering thank yous.

Laptops and kindles, rows of seats dotted with lethargic passengers.

Geometric architecture and lingering coffee beans, someone over there is having a cocktail. It's 5am.

Warped between places, and benign smiles, the airport is transgressed into a fluid reality. Human nature is a force to be reckoned with-

gestures waves expressions.

The quirks of moving and being not together but as single entities.

Each person derived by a longing to be left alone.

The air is thick and taunt, heads glancing at the arrivals board toying back down to reading or texting or staring at shoes.

Endless possibilities to define humanity exist here.

From suits to sun dresses, active wear, messy buns, blazers and mules. Diversity in abundance. That man over there-

he moves his hand on the tarmac

indicating friction,

uncertainty

sexual tension

mediocracy

or perhaps just traffic controlling.

Anatomy

TO SEE WITH EYES UNCLOUDED

At the optometrist they say

what can you see? instead of *can you see?*

It's as if they don't know the absurdity of that
question to someone who can taste colours.
Looking back I should have said;

I see cocaine showers whereas you might see scattered clouds.

I see razor blade stiches whereas you might see cycle tracks.

I see ragged hands itching inside my skin

I see everything

yet nothing at all.

MOTHER EARTH & MATARIKI GIVE BIRTH

Jealousy looks like tap water

running down the drain.

Greater stones are picked the ones that rise from the surf, laying their cheeks for moments on the sand, licking the broken ledge, climbing the cliffs, flicking the track.

Nights like these implode on the northern star they remind us of bigger things;

to look up, to have perception,

holding fast to hope far beyond our lifetime.

This dark anatomy is searched and questioned, shaken to reason,

held accountable for people's mishaps.

The milky way talks of connection, each fragment so precious in the scheme of things.

It begs us to ask; *What will you be? Who will you be?* These questions, they go unscathed.

Matariki is bright, a warming member swarming in dark anatomy.

She's cluster-focused, light-becoming, many worlds begin here.

So why we you blame her when things go wrong?

They say the natural world has faults, the only way out is punishment; to reap disaster upon her, to damage and unearth the magic between her legs -

until there's nothing left.

Only flaccid branches, polluted air, inches away from breaking down her womb.

I guess we have *the stars* to thank for that – or maybe just careless pricks.

BEDROOM STORIES

genuine laughs are like bedside cabinets

rigid, often useful on top but never *really* required

underneath.

It's not to say they're not quintessential in

providing convenience-

they just go unnoticed.

For millennials

a lumbered gloss surface

carries the reputation of being useless.

splinters lean in, smiling and nodding quietly

waiting on a hand to roll over touch the cigarette,

stow the inhaler, plug in the phone. with

maddening hunger smiles urge to be recognised.

everything aches for attention

god forbid it goes unnoticed.

A HOWL TO AMERICA

They're telling everyone to use guns.

They're saying – harm who you want, screw them all, show off your belligerent militia and have fun doing it!

They sit on mahogany chairs

with scotch on the rocks in stupid crystal tumblers bought

    using *exploitive* money *& Epstein wagers.*

They're saying – you don't deserve free healthcare, unprocessed food, living wages, housing, state security, your own uterus. Don't you get it?!

That *fucking* easy A

that stupid stamp on the globe with malicious *80-year-old senators.*

God forbid America, you sure have declared your own independence.

Is it too much to let people BREATHE life into this world?

Hell – you need an *ambush* of humanity.

Something to wake you from the dead.

WOOD BURNS

Wine is a floodgate for everything unwritten,

disturbing my peace

fire to philanthropy.

It's not enough to stay buried as a hatchet.

The drive thru at night-time is melancholic,

lights blink in slow motion

reminding me of better moments – a warm hug,
fire burning, family dinners.

The road is narrow and isolating,

 each man for themselves -

snatching paper bags and eyeing sad cheeseburgers.

How are we supposed to plan a life if we're always

carpe-dieming.

Look good feel good never really made sense until

flowers,

peace offerings mirroring a lack thereof.

The wind-up north tastes of syrup and watercress,

on Mondays it tastes

of stale concrete and disappointment.

Alas, these things take pieces of me

slowly wood-chipping and leaving me splintered.

THESE ARE THE THINGS THAT PARALYSE ME

Further to my email I must note that the creative realm is not one to be reckoned with.

The world of a glorified poet is not sparkling lights and clear skin, it is a deeply philosophical door that is shut behind them.

They come home from their meetings, obligations, and reserves to find a laptop blinking at them, waiting to catch them in a moment of solitude and torture the life out of them.

These documents and notebooks tell them how special they are, they reinforce their eye for the world as if it were literal.

If only writers wrote about the world as it is with all its mundane and expediential nonsense that could drive someone to die.

They write with such flair to encapsulate these
moments in extremity,

thinking too long about it, could in fact, drive you
to die.

So where do you begin?

Novelists, poets, and those alike alter our reality, so
we don't have to.

Suppressing the problems of the world is a
structural coincidence; glossing over the misery of
thousands of people just so two lovers can find
sense in their own meaningless context.

To what expense does their artificial prose impact on them?

That we don't know,

only empty bottles

cold rooms

and stacks of paper would tell you so.

2010

Covered in grass and cuts,

tangled hair and speckled daisies,

no concept of my own physicality, hanging from a

tree eating an apple around my missing front teeth.

To be unabashedly dorky and unashamedly hungry,

healthy and hearty, with just the right amount of

stamina

to explore until dusk.

Covered in bruises and stains, full of love and sweet

nectarines.

To feel this time stretch forever, flying through

books and laughs and falling into bed.

To love summer and insects and sweat and tears

playing spotlight

until eventually I didn't have to hide,

they had already found me.

POCKETS FULL OF POSIES

I'm going to unleash some slander in which I hope you'll interpret politically:

1. Lousy initiatives force us into malpractice.

2. *In libras libertas* oak trees are rebranded on bookshelves.

3. There is too much open space, clouded eyes and mulched leaves.

silk blood, velvet armour, and a fruity vest - that's what it takes to unhinge a conversation.

wet basketball shorts and a cold cocktail dress - that's what it takes to put a person away.

I read somewhere that a hit to the diagram is one of the worst blows, a spasming lung and wheezing chest is enough to curdle death. An abomination of sorts filter through our systems, nobody is safe, not

even from themselves.

Decrepit and in denial

the world stops on its axis,

pausing just for a moment

unfolding a lifetime.

PRADA BEST FRIEND

My best friend falls in love for the first time at 23,

stained red lips, teetered eyes

muffled sounds of

love rather than break.

She drifts naturally towards *prêt-à-porter*

meeting somewhere in between

terminally chic and ambitious complication.

Amber and coral

a laced bonnet, silk lining;

duty-calls to a square neck bodice,

low scoop back and complimentary straps.

An embellishing crime of charmeuse, enveloping

hands in satin.

A likened *Anna Wintour,* full of quiet discipline.

Briefly, she set designs a theatrical motion

bringing my reality to an almost crisp,

unused pointed lipstick

distilling a great artist in myself.

A folded tissue replaces conversation,

in awe of all things new, borrowed, and blue.

Melbourne is calling.

THIS BEAUTIFUL WORLD MUST BE SEARCHED

Colour your thinking in monstera flavoured leaves, let the grass ferment your sundried body.

Let them beg the questions: *Do you know who you are? Do you know what happened to you?*

Allow the bent daisies to repeat these things, until you devour the questions and dribble the answers out, like oil on a page. What if the meaning of life is a combination of production and distribution, those who command intimate attention and those who revolt the consequences?

The development of abstract and complex cultural forms, naturally rise and recede like the waves outside my home. Just like that, the meaning of life remains the same – to relish enjoyment and be amongst people. Dry upturned sycamore leaves, scuttle across the Peninsular, convincing me to run.

He holds my toes and strokes the under-turn of my foot, gesturing to the incoming cloud and the rain predicted from earlier. In this strange tableau, something comical yet equally as haunting, mists beyond us both. There are rocks shaped as people turning in the deep blue liquid lagoon. There is a child skipping over sand and screaming for his parents' attention.

Under a breath of wind, life embraces ordinariness, an ugly vulgarity imposed upon itself.

Perhaps in this moment, we are unaware, invulnerable to, untouched by; vulgarity and ordinariness; glancing at the deeper and tangible essence of life. The presence of life's magic is unforeseen, it is not all encompassing; it is small and finite. It *must* be searched, acknowledged, and *accepted* in its stagnant form.

LIFELINE

To love life, to love it even when

your stomach is in knots,

when everything has been

thrown, lacerated, and

relinquished into ash.

Even when loss sits on you, weighing you

down with cement until it covers every inch,

slowly taking your oxygen and leaving

you flat lining.

You think, *how can I survive this?*

but you do, you grab life like an ex-lover;

a cold limp hand, with cracks and configurations,

bony and shallow, and you say yes.

I will love you again.

Spring

POLLENATED MEN

He possessed a rudimentary intelligence,

countering ordinariness with maple hair and

weakness about the shoulders.

He spoke of the sky like it were his own,

his way of bearing mild inaptitude.

He loathed categories, considering himself more of

a

collective pollenated forecast.

Inept from categories and all-encompassing he was;

hazelnut catskins, cypress, fungal spores, and

especially damp indoors.

He spoke of adult things, yet I figured they needed

somewhere to go,

so, I absorbed them through my skin until they

crawled out of me.

He looked across at the sand dunes,

sprawled along a necklace of blue shore,

miles of surf

growing tough in hot wind.

Interrupted only by sharp cliffs, shrubs, and clay,

bent, overlooking, wearing the shape of the wind.

I admired his triviality, his knowledge about stars,

cheeks beaming with distorted light,

time speeding and bending around the two of us.

He fabricated my world as it curved, not because of

gravitational energy

but because I plummeted into his pillow,

thrusting deep into forgiveness

and a rudimentary man.

LUNCHTIME AROUSAL

A control fallacy is the body's way of going still.

Sincere compliments, lingering eyes, micro gestural brows, a gaze that explores, suggests, and leans closer.

Touch excuses itself from wetting one's lips,

shifting to display one's chest and shoulders,

thumbs through belt loops

and nearing the pelvis.

Pulling entices claiming,

deepening, growing more urgent.

Heavy breathing and whispering;

be mine.

Fumbling with the mesh top that feels restrictive,

anchored hands on the waist

convincing the skin to brush,

to keep on giving.

It's enough to direct eye contact,

to mirror body language,

to deplete all pragmatic decisions

and succumb to the bare minimum.

RAISE ME UP

I feel the cold in short bursts, wavering air, and

glares from down below.

Jittery, difficulty staying still,

veins jerking with each movement

and rolling over.

Speech seems to trail off, a noncommittal tension

all over.

Intensive staring with deep brown bark,

rustled birds hidden

and blocking shrubbery.

Darting eye contact, a budding conversationalist, a

leaf

bound

to fall.

MY OWN WORST CRITIC

Something in the margin

marvels at sweet monogamy.

Confirming importance and experimentalism,

there is a level of playfulness, a flickering tail

circling in transverse saucers.

These manuscripts are slender, wavering conviction

like they have the time,

thwarted reflections that mirror their writers -

giving me more than I bargained to know.

In these manuscripts, they demand to be talked

about;

pondered over in agonising detail

in the worst of times.

Kernels of intrigue bounce from each chapter,
alluring to a comma misplaced or excused
hyperbole. The grammar deals in both lies and
truths,

as if exploring the world ending

only to begin again the next morning.

In these manuscripts, there is a tightness in voice,
speaking to the point with an intense stare.
Sentences hang off the edge

their rancid wet lips

thinning, halting, shattering.

The only way I can bring myself to view these
manuscripts, is to awaken every wolf and monster
that sleeps inside of me.

What a shame to wear the skin of a gentle human
who undervalues what I think.

THE MORNING AFTER

The blood of the morning rises too bright through my window shades.

I fell asleep wrapped in warm sugar,

awoken by the harsh cold,

numb

canoodling in self-pity.

Scouring for a teacup in a room cordoned by empty bottles,

an ashtray, leaflets of last week's newspaper.

Souring through lumpy swallows, urging for a static soda,

anything to harden the regrets from last night.

The sheets, now scattered with toast crumbs,

itch their way onto my thighs, multiplying with each turnover.

Nihilistic irony floats from my curtains

onto my forehead, remnants of last night swirl
around

like lyric activism.

This hall is narrow and empty

I'm learning to shy away from complexity,

the kind that comes in a bottle and tastes of burnt
tequila.

The cold hard truth is that I cannot,

in fact, eat my theoretical concepts

and wash it down with a Lexapro.

Scorched memories of a rendezvous,

now tainted by a thin and protruding body,

flailing under covers,

unable to cease the day.

LITTLE WOMEN

thrust together

chests touching

pelvis grazing mine.

swelling in all the right places,

whereas men were flat.

a bodily craving of more, of wanting to be nearer,

a want to be on one another

indefinitely.

without any roughness, a plump smoothness,

peace and safety.

an equal attempt at using our body's force,

without harm.

lilac powder catching the air between us

vanilla drifting and fusing the space around us.

a haven of sweetness

with dribbles of sultry,

I can hear the cheers from all the women who

came before us.

AIRPORT SECRETS

Are airports another segment of class division and

hidden tax fraud?

They either walk too fast,

walk too slow,

stare at their phones,

or stare right at each other.

Dressed for communion

or for the streets,

regal or ruined; an absurd monogamy of people

unite here.

It's as if by choice and coincidence, that the world

opens a transcendent portal,

a short space for people of multiple classes to

engage in tax fraud.

In the cradle of renaissance herself,

passengers lose their younger days in time vessels,

as lines grow on starch faces.

GROCERY SHOPPING

Feminine sensibilities are kinder, more fragile

the same way kauri twirls toward the sky and

flattens into paper.

Deep in the supermarket, it's quiet heart murmurs

to the sound of packets.

Walls around us,

watching our breathe melt away into

rows of tin,

running along lights.

The business of this place is the acquisition of

verdure

and tinned tomatoes.

The air is still and asthmatic,

plausible moments are tied together and hung from

my wrist,

a charm bracelet of life's inequities.

SUMMER

The city is baking,

asphalt sizzles and children echo from the suburbs
– cries of ice-cream and forgotten towels.

Owlish eyes meet under verandas, smiling good-
naturedly – as if by routine.

Each gap filling with frantic chatter, cars steaming
forward

gripping the sweating curb.

In another world, children's blood sweat and tears
are dripping from jeans.

In confined heat, abuse and owlish eyes meet.

As if by routine, they grip wooden seats and play
piano on the sewing machines.

Hardened by a rough and untamed atmosphere –
human rights are diminished.

A LETTER FROM MANUKA TERRACE

We settled in the tussocks

beneath the nasally Mackenzie country,

governed by stratus clouds hanging loose like

Christmas baubles.

In the evenings, sea gulls made an ecstatic

calligraphy against the gloom,

landing on cobble stones and neat outlines.

I could see the moths mistake something like

blaring headlines in the dark,

for home.

Dust bulldozed overhead, remnants of rain skating

down.

Nursing a Pinot Gris, I wrapped myself in your

mother's antique quilt.

Only hills molested this near-nothingness, old
records glossing over the swell,

the mapping of something happening inside of me.

In the morning we woke to the hum of distant
mosquitoes, dressed in composites and aluminium-
the shrieking rich on their safari over the alps.

I still faintly remember the sound of gravel
crunching, the Navara entering without fear,

this I hear still exists in my memory.

The cold hypnosis of the water's edge, a penetrable
onyx of being misunderstood and diaphanous. The
lake retained a unity unlike anything other than the
sky, a merging like a subordinate clause whose
designs are not kind.

So perhaps I don't even mean the lake anymore,
but an experience of being in two places at once,
which syllable by syllable I make the mistake of
displacing.

www.ingramcontent.com/pod-product-compliance
Lightning Source LLC
Chambersburg PA
CBHW050004070726
47592CB00018B/786